A Beachcomber's Journal

A Beachcomber's Journal

Seonaid McGurk

ISBN: 978-1-78324-268-9

Published and Book design by
www.wordzworth.com

CONTENTS

Foreword to A Beachcomber's Journal   vii

Acknowledgements   ix

Map of Monifieth Beach and Buddon   xi

Introduction   1

Bottles and Glassware   5

Messages In Bottles   35

Vulcanised Rubber Stoppers, Glass/Ceramic Stoppers and Bottle Tops   41

Pottery   53

Plastic   55

Unusual Finds   71

Nature   79

Tiny Finds   85

Brewers And Drinks Manufacturers   87

Author Bio   89

FOREWORD TO A BEACHCOMBER'S JOURNAL

It is my pleasure to write this foreword to a book which I have, for some time, encouraged the author to write in order to share with a wider audience the fruits of both her beach walks and her research into what she has found on them. We tend to think of a beachcomber as being someone who walks along beaches looking for objects of value and perhaps making a living from them. The material found and described in this most welcome book however, is not of monetary value but is of great value in terms of shedding light on aspects of social and economic history.

Finds are grouped into types and are presented in order of discovery from 2018 to early 2022 along with illustrations and the results of research into them. The information and stories related to the finds are both fascinating and educational. The glass bottles particularly reveal so much about their production and contents which in turn reveal, for example, what people in the recent past were eating (Worcestershire Sauce), drinking (Stillade soft drinks) or putting on their hair (Brylcreem).

The true value of this work lies above all in that it is very much a personal view and commentary highlighting some of the issues facing the marine environment today. It is shocking now to see the amount of plastic bottles, food wrappers and other detritus that washes up on our beaches with the potential to cause so much harm to the environment generally and to marine creatures in particular. There is an ever-increasing popular desire to enjoy the great outdoors and we should all heed the book's advice about taking our own litter home to dispose of safely and note the given details of British Divers Marine Life Rescue, the rescue organisation to contact if an injured or distressed marine mammal is found.

Perhaps there is a bit of beachcomber in all of us and this book demonstrates the variety of material that can be found on our shores and the potential wealth of information research into it can reveal. It should also encourage us to appreciate the natural beauty we are surrounded by and to take responsibility for our interactions with the environment. I hope this is the first book of its kind and the results of further beachcombing might follow in due course.

Lisbeth M Thoms

MBE HonFSAScot

ACKNOWLEDGEMENTS

I would like to thank everyone who has contributed to this book, especially the encouragement from my family and friends to actually start writing and then keep going ....

Thank you to my youngest son, Kieran, who has been invaluable in helping me with the technical side of bringing it all together, my eldest son, Danny, for some of the photography and advice regarding British Divers Marine Life Rescue protocols, my husband, Kevin, who has put up with me carrying all sorts of "treasure" home, for taking the cover photograph and Shelby, our Border Collie, who has been my constant companion on many beach walks.

Special thanks to Lisbeth Thoms MBE HonFSAScot for writing the foreword, proof reading and for providing invaluable advice throughout the entire process of writing this book. I am deeply indebted.

I would also like to thank everyone else who has contributed, either by giving me permission to use photographs, their images or by passing on their finds for me to research. It is all greatly appreciated.

(Photograph courtesy of Kris Auchinleck)

This picture was taken in 2013 when I discovered a section of jawbone on the beach.

Also, in the picture is my very dear friend and First Aid colleague, David Pullen, who gave over 60 years of service to St Andrew's First Aid. We did many beach cleans together as first aid duties. Sadly, Dave passed away in March 2019 but I often think of him when I am on the beach. Caroline and Sandy Smith, pictured with us, are two of our regular Eco Force beach cleaners.

MAP OF MONIFIETH BEACH AND BUDDON

The map below (not to Ordnance Survey standards!) is to give an indication of where most of my finds are located as I log the area in which they are found, along with the date and details of what I have collected.

Section No 1 covers the area from where the Dighty Water runs into the Tay just east of Balmossie Station to the Monifieth Burn outfall to the south of the Blue Seaway Park in Monifieth.

Section No 2 is from the east side of the Monifieth Burn outfall to where the Buddon Burn meets the sea. The vast majority of my finds have come from this section. Access to part of the beach in this section is dependent on the firing times published by the MOD and the tides.

Section No 3 is from the east side of the Buddon Burn along towards the two lighthouses at Buddon Ness and beyond towards Carnoustie. Access to Section 3 is also restricted by firing times.

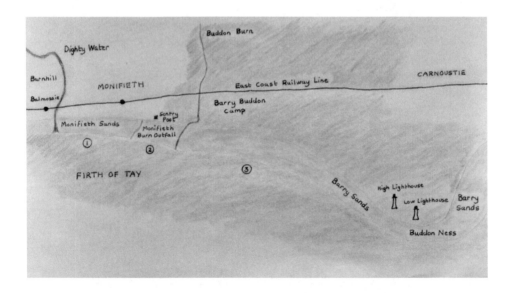

INTRODUCTION

My childhood days were spent in Glenesk, Angus, miles away from the sea. During the school holidays I spent time with my younger sister, my Mum and her late husband, the Yorkshire naturalist, ornithologist, writer and TV presenter, Michael Clegg. Michael had a shed down beside the foreshore at Westhaven, Carnoustie, until the mid 1980s, where we spent many happy hours on the beach collecting shells, looking in rock pools and walking.

Later on, when they lived in Knaresborough in North Yorkshire, they had a caravan at Kilnsea, just at the base of the Spurn Peninsula at the mouth of the River Humber. It was a wonderful place to escape to – no electricity, gas lamps and water pumped in from a bottle outside. It was completely relaxing. The coastline there is absolutely fascinating as huge gun emplacements from World War 2 have crashed (literally) onto the beach over the years due to the erosion of the boulder clay underneath. The original caravan pitch is now long gone, along with the toilet block and the coastguard tower which also stood close by. Spurn Point is now an island as the road leading all the way out to the point washed away several years ago. The beach is great for fossil hunt-

Michael's former shed, March 2020

ing. Sadly, this erosion has seen the disappearance of homes, villages, farming land and communities all along the east coast of Yorkshire and seems to be accelerating.

In 1994, after having lived in Dundee for 9 years, my husband, Kevin, our son Danny who was a year old and I moved to Monifieth, some 6 miles to the east of Dundee. Our second son, Kieran was born in 1995. The beach was, at that time, rocky and the path along the sea front had fallen onto the beach. It wasn't the best or easiest place to walk along with two young children. However, over the years the path was reinstated as part of the Sustrans cycle network and with the construction of sea defences, sand started to build up and reform the beach. The water in the Firth of Tay was cleaned up after the installation of water treatment works. The variety of shells washed up on the beach, feeding sea birds, seals and dolphins would now indicate a much healthier ecosystem. Unfortunately, like the east coast of Yorkshire, erosion would appear to be speeding up here as well. The Monifieth Burn and the Buddon Burn are constantly rerouting and changing course. Tidal surges are becoming more common and one in December 2020 ripped out a 6-metre-wide swathe of marram grass along the shore towards the Buddon Burn in one fell swoop, as well as flooding the reed beds behind the dunes. It is an ever changing and fascinating landscape.

I first became involved with Monifieth Eco Force's beach cleans around 2012 as a member of St Andrew's First Aid as it was one of our duties to provide first aid cover to the volunteer beach cleaners. Ironically, I think I was also the first casualty after cutting my finger on a piece of marram grass!

The Eco Force volunteers meet on the first Saturday of every month at the kiosk at the Blue Seaway Park, Monifieth, throughout the year and also take part in the twice-yearly Barry Buddon cleans in conjunction with the Rotary Club. If there is no live firing at the Barry Buddon Ranges, the volunteers clean the stretch from the Barry Buddon Burn to the Dighty Water at Balmossie. Due to the lockdown enforced in 2020 because of the Covid 19 Pandemic, beach cleans were temporarily suspended until restrictions were eased enough to allow them to resume.

A little bit of history …

The Dundee to Arbroath railway was opened in 1838 but the track gauge was only standardised in 1848 so that it could connect to the rest of the emerging Scottish railway system. In December 1905, the first Dundee to Monifieth tram made its way along the line, the initial fare being the princely sum of 4p. (Source: Monifieth Local History Society). This meant that more people were able to come from further afield to enjoy a day out at the seaside at a reasonable cost.

Watching horses racing along the beach drew considerable crowds during Victorian times until 1841. By the 1930s, motor racing and motor cycle racing were popular pursuits on the sands. It was also possible to take an aerial flight round the Monifieth Bay for 5 shillings, with the planes taking off and landing on the beach. At the end of the day, the wings were folded up on the planes and they were pushed through the tunnel under the railway line to Crichton's garage in Tay Street for storage.

(Source: "Old Broughty Ferry and Monifieth by A W Brotchie and J J Herd)

These days the bay is a big draw for kite surfers and also, since the Covid 19 pandemic, a destination for open water swimmers. It is also very popular with dog walkers and horse riders as well as families.

We are incredibly fortunate to have this beautiful coastline on our doorstep, but we need to do all we can to protect and preserve it for the wildlife and future generations.

It is amazing what you can find washed up, in amongst what appears on the face of it, to be a pile of rubbish. With a little detective work some items have a big back story, others perhaps less so but which are still interesting.

BOTTLES AND GLASSWARE

Depending on the tides, there is sometimes a lot of glass on the beach, most of it broken, but whole bottles do also turn up. Broken glass was also an issue in the early 20th century as St Andrew's Ambulance Association first aiders were on duty every weekend on the beach to provide first aid to the people who came to spend the day at the seaside. The records (in beautiful copperplate handwriting) indicate that many people were treated for cuts to their feet.

In May 2019 I was lucky enough to find three whole bottles, tucked behind a log. Left to right, they are Robertsons Fruit Products of Dundee, Lambs Strathmore Springs, Forfar and Wright of Perth.

Robertsons Fruit Products Ltd had an incorporation date of 2 June 1938.

Robertsons bottled Dextora (a glucose drink) and Pola Cola at their factory at 12 Corso Street, Dundee. They were taken over by Strathmore Springs in the 1970s.

(Source: retrodundee.blogspot)

I have several Robertsons Fruit Products bottles in my collection, 2 of which were found sealed with Sun Joy stoppers. They also produced Stillade in a variety of flavours.

J Lamb, Brewer and Bottler, was based at West High Street, Forfar, in 1899.

(Source: Scottish Post Office Directories, Forfar Directory and Year Book 1899)

The Registered Design No 783665 indicates a registration date between 1933 and 1934.

John Wright & Co (Perth) Ltd was a brewing and bottling company based at 18 North Methven Street, Perth. It was founded around 1700 and was registered in 1925. It was acquired by Vaux Breweries in 1961.

(Source: breweryhistory.com)

Avon Cologne Bottle
January 2020

This bottle is marked "Avon" with a US Patent Number 103048 and "Made in the USA". It was designed by Frank Earl Higgins and was patented in 1937 on 2nd February for a term of 14 years.

Art Deco Style Bottle With Lid
February 2020

The base is marked 779139 which indicates it was produced in 1932-1933. As it has a wide neck, it may have been for food use.

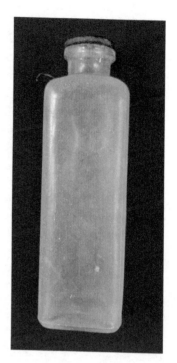

Small Bottle With Rubber Stopper

I haven't been able to find anything out about this little bottle, but it is cute at only 10 cms high. It may have contained medication of some sort given the size and would have stood neatly on a shelf as it is rectangular in shape.

Bottles and Brylcreem Jar
February 2020

This eclectic collection was found on one walk following Storm Ciara which hit at the beginning of February 2020. It is quite unusual to find so many whole bottles. The collection includes a Forthill Dairy milk bottle with 1949 on the base, two wine bottles, a mineral water bottle, a medicine bottle which would have had a cork or glass stopper and finally a Brylcreem jar. Brylcreem is a men's hair styling product, first created in 1928. The numbers on the base, 859194, indicate that the design was registered in 1949. Originally the lid would have been black but the colour has rubbed off over the intervening years. I have found several Brylcreem jars since. They have British Design Registry Date numbers indicating that they date from the 1930s.

Forthill Dairy Farm was situated on Forthill Road, Broughty Ferry and is shown on the Ordnance Survey Map Sheet No 4631 , 1:2500 scale, published in 1954. The site is now a housing development.

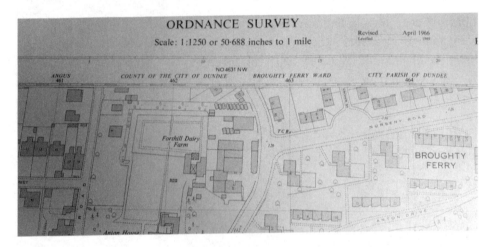

Walker's Kilmarnock Whisky bottle
March 2020

I found this bottle beside the Buddon Burn. John Walker, 1805-1857, as a teenager, managed a grocery and wine and spirits store in Kilmarnock High Street. By 1825 he was dealing mainly in whisky and blending made to order whiskies. Eventually he did use his own name, establishing Walker's Kilmarnock Whisky as a brand.

The glass itself is full of bubbles and the seam lines are visible on the sides of the bottle. Part of the original cork is still inside. John Walker's son, Alexander, introduced the square bottle in 1860, the logic behind the square design being easier transportation and fewer breakages.

(Source: Wikipedia)

**G Thomson & Son, Falkirk,
Thomson Craik & Co, Perth,
Usher Bottle
March 2020**

G Thomson & Son, Falkirk

This bottle, found at Buddon, has Falkirk, Airdrie and Dysart embossed on the side of the bottle. The vulcanised rubber stopper is in very good condition. James Calder & Co (Brewers) Ltd, The Shore Brewery, Alloa, took over G Thomson & Son in 1950.

*(Source: The Brewing Industry: A Guide to Historical Records,
Lesley Richmond, Alison Turton)*

Thomson, Craik & Co, Perth

Thomson, Craik & Co were based in Glover Street, Perth and described as aerated water manufacturers and bottlers in the Scottish Post Office Directories dated 1907-1908. The firm of W B Thomson Ltd (wholesale, retail wine and spirits business, South Street, Perth) decided to spin off their aerated water business and merge it with John Craik & Co of Perth in the early 1900s thus forming the business Thomson, Craik & Co Ltd. This business was subsequently acquired by John Wright & Co (Perth) Ltd which was the biggest brewery firm in Perthshire. The business eventually closed in the late 1980s. The plastic screw cap would date this particular bottle to the 1960s/70s.

(Source: breweryhistory.com)

Usher Bottle

Thomas Usher & Son founded their brewery at 106 St Leonard's Street, Edinburgh, in 1817. It was acquired by James Usher & Cunningham in 1831 and moved to the

Park Brewery in 1860. It was subsequently acquired by Vaux Breweries in 1959. The name was changed to Ushers Brewery in 1972. It was sold again in 1980 to Allied Breweries and ceased brewing in 1981.

(Source: breweryhistory.com)

Ballingall & Son Ltd bottle
21 March 2020

Unfortunately, the neck of this bottle had been fairly recently broken off but the writing along the side was worthy of further investigation. The Park and Pleasance Breweries in Dundee were founded before 1750 and acquired by William Ballingall in 1844. He died in 1856 and his son Hugh, who was apparently only 16 at the time, took over the business. Hugh was elected as provost in 1884. The Park and Pleasance Breweries buildings are shown on the 1:2500 Ordnance Survey Map of 1954 on the south side of Lochee Road, Dundee, on the aptly named Hop Street. The Lower Pleasance and Park Street are both nearby. Brewing ceased in 1964.

(Source: breweryhistory.com)

John Robertson & Son, Dundee & Perth bottle January 2020

According to the Scottish Post Office Directories of 1903-1904, John Robertson & Son manufactured aerated water at 21 North Tay Street, Dundee.

The bottle itself was manufactured by United Glass Bottles and has a registered design number 761530 which would date it to 1931.

The United Glass Bottle Manufacturers Ltd was formed in 1913 when Ravenhead Glass, Cannington, Shaw & Co, Nuttall Co, Alfred Alexander & Co and Robert Candlish & Son came together to raise enough capital to buy rights in the first successful automated bottle making machine invented by Michael Owens who founded Owens-Illinois Inc.

Production was subsequently concentrated at a newly built factory at Charlton and 2 in St Helens. They primarily produced bottles until 1931 when they diversified into producing bowls, jugs and glasses for the domestic market.

In 1937 the company acquired the bottle manufacturing subsidiaries of several distilling companies including James Buchanan & Co, John Dewar & Sons, John Haig & Co, Tanqueray Gordon & Co, John Walker & Sons and other associated companies. In 1959 the company changed its name to United Glass Ltd. Many of the bottles in my collection bear the UGB stamp on the base.

An advertisement from 1922 states that the company manufactured a staggering 250,000,000 bottles per annum and was the largest bottle manufacturing company in Europe.

(Source: Grace's Guide to British Industrial History)

Scottish Brewers Ltd Bottle
8 March 2020

This bottle is complete with its vulcanised rubber stopper. Scottish Brewers Ltd was formed from a merger of William McEwen & Co Ltd and William Younger & Co Ltd, both based in Edinburgh. The brewery was closed in April 1960.

(Source: breweryhistory.com)

Brylcreem Bottle
30 March 2020

The British Registry Date Numbers indicate that this bottle is from 1930 (758455 on the cap).

Goodall Backhouse & Co Bottles
2 April 2020 and July 2020

Robert Goodall (1831-1870) had a chemist's shop in Leeds and started making Yorkshire Relish from a family recipe using shallots, soy sauce, garlic, malt vinegar and 27 spices. He subsequently went into business with two chemists, Henry Backhouse and William Powell, in 1858; the firm being known as Goodall Backhouse & Co. By 1874 it was the biggest sauce manufacturer in the world. Goodall Backhouse & Co was eventually sold to Hammonds Sauce Co in 1959.

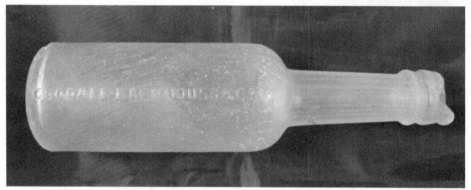

(Source: letslookagain.com)

The bottles would have been sealed with glass stoppers, similar to the ones I have found. The opaque bottle has obviously been in the wars over the years, sustaining some damage to the neck.

Art Deco bottle
3 April 2020

This pretty little bottle would appear to have had cologne in it. The design would suggest that it dates to around the 1930s. It is 9 cms high.

Johnstone Hill & Co Ltd
18 April 2020

The firm of Johnstone Hill & Co Ltd, Aerated Water Manufacturers, was based at the Old Brewery, Buccleuch Street, Dumfries.

The company of W G Johnstone & Co at the same address is listed in the 1911-1912 Scottish Post Office Directories, Dumfries and District.

Coca Cola Bottle
1 May 2020

The distinctive contoured bottle shape was developed in 1916. This bottle is heavy for its size.

(Source: Collecting Old Coca Cola Bottles by Kate Miller-Wilson, Antique Collector)

Spout Bottle
1 May 2020

This small bottle (12 cms) has a tiny spout on the neck. It has a screw top fitting. The Registered Design Number is 817802 which dates it to 1937.

Brylcreem Jar
18 May 2020

The Registered Design Number on this jar is 877553 which indicates it was registered in 1955/1956. The lid is still the original colour and is quite intact. It seems to have been a very popular hair styling product as I have found several of these jars over the years.

Tiny Bottle
18 May 2020

This tiny bottle is only 7.5 cms high, complete with resident shell, is made of very thick glass which is full of bubbles. It doesn't sit squarely on its base either. As an educated guess, it probably dates to around 1900 or even earlier.

Boots Bottle
24 May 2020

I found this at Buddon following a very high tide which had swept a lot of the old rubbish back out to sea. The screw cap is quite fragile, and the bottle is abraded, so it has been in the sea/on the beach for quite some time.

Specifique Lancelot Paris Bottle
26 May 2020

This pretty little octagonal bottle in orange glass was half buried in the sand on Monifieth Beach. It is moulded glass with little bubbles through it. In spite of the helpful (or so I thought) writing along the side, I have been unable to find out anything about it. Orange glass is quite rare. It is only 9.5 cms long.

Melville & Co, Dundee Bottle
July 2020

I haven't been able to find any information on this company. If anyone knows anything about Melville & Co, please let me know.

DPM Milk Bottle
30 July 2020

Dundee Pasteurised Milk Co had several shops serving the city in the 1960s and 1970s, including Lochee High Street, Craigiebank, Dura Street, Perth Road, Dundonald Street, Princes Street, Fintry Road, Union Street, Blackness Road and Arbroath Road, plus a cafe in Reform Street. Their headquarters were in Mains Road. The company was no longer trading by 1974.

(Source: Retro Dundee)

Stephenson Brothers Furniture Cream Bottle
1 August 2020

The Stephenson Group was formed in 1856 in Bradford, Yorkshire, and originally produced soap-based agents for wool processing along with furniture polish and wax.

(Source: Company History/Stephenson)

This bottle dates to around 1908, when glass was starting to supersede stoneware.

Part of the original stopper is inside the bottle.

(Source: whatthevictoriansthrewaway.com)

James Calder, Alloa, Bottle and Stopper/Fowler, Prestonpans, Bottle and Stopper
1 April 2020

James Calder acquired the Shore Brewery, Whins Road, Alloa, in 1862. Brewing ceased in 1921.

(Source: breweryhistory.com)

The stopper has a bee embossed in the middle.

John Fowler & Co Ltd was founded around 1720 at High Street, Prestonpans, and was registered in 1865. It was acquired by Northern Breweries of Great Britain Ltd in 1960. Brewing ceased in 1962. I think this bottle must be over 100 years old as the glass is very thick, heavy and full of bubbles. It also has visible side seams.

(Source: breweryhistory.com)

Hays Bottle
August 2020

Wm Hay & Sons had a mineral water works at College Street in Aberdeen and also at Beverley Road, Inverurie.

The company was incorporated on 23 March 1938.

They produced a wide range of aerated drinks including Ginger Champagne, Sherbet, Seltzer Water, Hop Ale and Ginger Beer, to name but a few, as well as unfermented fruit wines and cordials. They also had a "latest speciality" in one of their advertisements: "Hay's Dazzle Beer."

(Source: doriccolumns.wordpress)

Strathmore Springs, Forfar and Manchester Bottle
August 2020

This bottle is a curious one, bearing Forfar and Manchester on the shoulder of the bottle. I have found no reference to Manchester when researching Strathmore Springs.

The base of the bottle is marked "D. B & Co Ld" which was the company Dunn Bennett & Co (Ltd) c. 1875-1983, manufacturing earthenwares at Hanley then Burslem. In 1968 it became part of the Royal Doulton Group.

(Source: thepotteries.org)

Robert Younger Ltd, Edinburgh Bottle
September 2020

Robert Younger Ltd was based at St Anne's Brewery, 60 Abbeyhill, Edinburgh. It was founded in 1854 and registered in 1896. As the case with so many smaller breweries, it was acquired by Scottish Brewers Ltd on 1 March 1961 and brewing subsequently ceased.

(Source: breweryhistory.com)

Campbell & Co, Forfar
September 2020

Campbell & Co were aerated water manufacturers, listed in the 1911 edition of The Forfar Directory and Yearbook.

John Campbell, Perth Bottle
October 2020

This beautifully coloured bottle is still in excellent condition and is made of very thick glass which is full of bubbles. John Campbell manufactured aerated waters, fruit wines, cordials and confectionery at Feus Road, Perth. It weighs 750g – most other bottles typically weigh around 600g. Aqua glass was typical from the late 19th century through to the 1920s. As this bottle had the neck added after the body of the bottle had been made, this would indicate that it pre-dates 1880.

(Source: Scottish Post Office Directories, Perth, 1885-1912)

This is also a John Campbell bottle but not quite as attractive as the one above. This example was found in December 2021.

Whitbread Bottles
7 October 2020

This damaged bottle is very dark in colour and quite heavy.

Whitbread's Brewery was founded in 1742 by Samuel Whitbread at Old Street, St Luke's, London, moving to Chiswell Street in 1750.

(Source: www.gla.ac.uk)

The stopper doesn't belong to bottle even though they were found together. I have been unable to identify the origins of the stopper.

D & W Edwards, Broughty Ferry, Bottle
9 October 2020

D & W Edwards were porter and ale bottlers and also manufactured horehound beer in Church Street/Princes Street, Broughty Ferry in 1900-1901. They were listed in the Scottish Post Office Directories 1905-1906 as aerated water manufacturers based at Camperdown Street, Broughty Ferry. The Ordnance Survey Map, Dundee Burgh East Const 1953 NO 4350 indicates "Aerated water works" at the west end of Camperdown Street.

The base of the bottle has "K B Ld", "C" and 1139 on it. John Kilner began operating glass plants in Yorkshire in 1842 until 1937. Kilner Brothers Ltd was the last named of the 4 Kilner companies and was liquidated in 1937 with the patents and trademarks being sold on to United Glass Bottle Manufacturers the same year

There was a bottling plant at Thornhill Lees, Dewsbury, 1873-1920 and one at Conisbrough, Doncaster, 1873-1937. The "C" would indicate that this bottle was manufactured at the Conisbrough site.

(Source: Grace's Guide to British Industrial History)

I believe this bottle to date from the early twentieth century as it is heavy for its size, full of bubbles and with visible side seams. Other than being a bit abraded, it is in remarkably good condition.

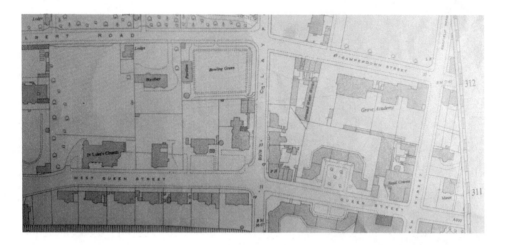

Foster Clark Ltd Maidstone Bottle
19 Nov 2020

I found this bottle on the beach at Broughty Ferry, partially buried in the sand. George Foster Clark and his brothers, William and Henry, launched their grocery sundries business in 1891 as Foster Clark & Co. The company of Foster Clark Ltd was registered in 1910 so this bottle is after this date. The Eiffel Tower was erected in Paris in 1889 and George Foster registered the name as his lemonade trademark. It proved a wise move as the name Foster Clark and the trade name "Eiffel Tower" became household words. The early bottles also had a picture of the Eiffel Tower embossed on them.

(Source: Foster Clark's 1891 to 1965)

The bottle is only 10.5 cms tall and contained crystals which were mixed with boiling water to make the "Eiffel Tower Lemonade" syrup which was then diluted with water.

(Source: doyouremember.co.uk – Food and Drink)

Heinz 57 Octagonal Bottle with Screw Cap
November 2020

This bottle dates from the 1930s. There were many brightly coloured advertisements at the time, one proudly proclaiming it was 'The Favourite Ketchup of 110 nations.'

(Source: chronicallyvintage.com)

J L & Co LD C Bottle
December 2020

J L & Co Ld is the firm of John Lumb & Co which operated from 1870 to 1905 as J L & Co then as J L & Co Ld from 1905 to 1937 when the firm became a limited partnership. The "C" denotes the factory at Castleford, West Yorkshire. It subsequently became part of United Glass in 1937.

(Source: sha.org>bottle, Bill Lockhart, Beau Shriver, Bill Lindsey and Carol Serr)

Mustard Jar
December 2020

This jar was manufactured by Forsters Glass Co which was based at Atlas Glass Works in St Helens, Lancashire, from 1878 to 1966, when it was taken over by Rockwell Glass.

(Source: Grace's Guide to Industrial History)

Despite an extensive search online, I have been unable to find out who made the mustard (not Colmans!) or when it is dated from. I can make out 'LADY' on the top of the strapline and 'WHAT YOU WANT' underneath.

Tizer Bottle with
Bakelite Screw Cap, Buddon
25 December 2020

This bottle has a registered design number 869908 which indicates that it was produced in the early 1950s. The Tizer brand was acquired by A G Barr in 1972.

(Source: Wikipedia: A G Barr PLC)

Dettol Bottle RD 776068
November 2020

This bottle design was registered between 1932 and 1933. It has a tablespoons scale down one side and a teaspoon scale down the other.

R Douglas Ltd Bottle
with 1925 Stopper
January 2021

R Douglas Ltd had a factory at Lothrie Works, Weymssfield, in Kirkcaldy.

In 1911, they opened a new factory producing aerated water in Townhill Road, Dunfermline.

(Source: douglashistory.co.uk/
www.dunfermlineheritage.org)

The business was acquired by A G Barr (the makers of Irn Bru) in 1963.

(Source: The Douglas Archives)

Robert Barr Ltd Bottle
with Bakelite Screw Cap
January 2021

Robert Barr started a soft drinks business in 1875 in Burnfoot Lane, Falkirk. His son, Robert Fulton Barr, began a second business in Glasgow in 1887 which was then taken over in 1892 by his brother, Andrew Greig Barr (A G Barr). Barr's 'Iron Brew' was launched in 1901. Andrew was only 31 when he died in 1903.

A G Barr became a limited company in 1904. His younger brother, William Snodgrass Barr, took over as chairman until 1931, when he handed the chairmanship to his nephew, Colonel Robert Barr.

In 1947, 'Iron Brew' was renamed 'Irn Bru'. The company was floated on the Stock Exchange in 1965.

(Source: agbarr.co.uk)

David Nicoll, Fleuchar Craig, Dundee
17 January 2021

This business was listed in the 1896 Dundee Directory as David Nicoll, Aerated Water Manufacturer, Fleuchar Craig Works, Dundee. The factory was in Scott Street, Dundee, and is shown in the OS Map Second Edition 1903, Forfarshire Sheet LIV 5, 1:2500 scale.

An advertisement in the Scottish Post Office Directory for Dundee 1899-1900 stated that the business had been established for over 40 years as manufacturers of high class aerated water, British wines a speciality and brewers of non-intoxicating beer and stout.

The water was sourced from the Logie Spout Springs.

This bottle's stopper was held on by a wire running from the stopper into the neck of the bottle.

(Source: National Library of Scotland, Dundee Directory)

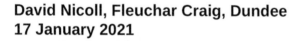

R T Ramsay, Hillside Dairy, Dundee
22 January 2021

I have been unable to find out anything about this milk bottle other than an article which appeared in the Dundee "Courier" newspaper, dated 5 January 1945, stating that customers who failed to return their empty bottles would no longer receive deliveries.

I am guessing that after several years of the Second World War raging that raw materials for the manufacture of new glass were in very short supply, hence the article in the "Courier".

It is in very good condition.

Green Bottle
22 January 2021

When I first spotted this in the sand, I thought it was a broken bottle neck, not a whole bottle. It is only 8.5 cms tall and would have been sealed with a cork.

As it is so small and in green glass, I suspect it may have contained poison of some description.

Scott's Emulsion Bottle
15 February 2021

Scott's Emulsion was first marketed in 1876 by Alfred B Scott and Samuel Bowne in New York, following 3 years of experimenting to produce a more palatable version of cod liver oil.

(Source: oldmainartifacts.wordpress.com)

It was extensively advertised and was reputed to be effective in treating tuberculosis, bronchitis, coughs and colds among other maladies. It is still produced today, bearing the Scott's Emulsion name by GlaxoSmithKline.

(Source: Bay Bottles)

Round Bottle with Silver Lid
15 February 2021

This pretty little bottle is only 7 cms tall. I think it would have contained perfume or cologne as is small enough to pop in a handbag.

G & P Barrie Ltd, Glasgow
January 2021

G & P Barrie Ltd were based at 191 Albert Street, Dundee. The business was established in 1830. Their bottling plant was situated at 181 Clepington Road, Dundee and closed down in April 1983. They manufactured Sunspan in orange, lemon and cola flavours.

(Source: retrodundee.blogspot.com)

They also had a factory in Maxwell Road, Pollockshields, Glasgow, manufacturing fruit wines, cordials, aerated water and also brewed non-intoxicating bitter beer, stout and ginger beer.

(Source: Scottish Post Office Directory, Glasgow 1904-1905)

This bottle is sealed with a chisel shaped stopper rather than the more usual circular screw top.

Mitchell, Dunfermline and Bathgate
27 February 2021

William Nicoll Mitchell began his working life with Robert Douglas Ltd, Aerated Water Manufacturers in Kirkcaldy and was appointed as manager at their new factory in Dunfermline in 1911. After being passed over for the manager's job at the Kirkcaldy headquarters, he set up his own business.

W N Mitchell & Sons Ltd, Aerated Water Manufacturers, began business in North Berwick in 1936 and relocated to 43 Pilmuir Street, Dunfermline, in 1938. In 1970 the business moved to an 18,000 square feet purpose built factory at Garvock Hill, Dunfermline.

In late 1992 production was moved to Woodrow's factory at Pitreavie Business Park, Dunfermline. Woodrow took over the Mitchell Business in April 1993.

(Source: dunfermlineheritage.org)

Garvie, Milngavie
27 February 202

Garvie's soft drinks factory was situated at Allander Road and Sinclair Street, Milngavie, from 1959, producing a wide range of carbonated drinks including cream soda and cider in the 1960s and 70s. They delivered their goods to Glasgow and the west of Scotland. The factory was demolished in 2002.

(Source: www.trailsandtales.org)

Unmarked Brown Glass Bottle with Vulcanised Rubber Stopper
3 April 2021

I found this bottle lying in the reed beds past the Buddon sentry post during the April 2021 beach clean. It is unusual in that there is no embossing on the bottle nor the vulcanised rubber stopper. I believe it to date from the Second World War as the stopper is showing signs of wear due to the poorer quality rubber. Also, because the bottle is unmarked, it could be returned to any brewery to be reused, unlike all of the other bottles in my collection which can be traced directly back to the original brewery or soft drinks manufacturer.

Bovril Jar
May 2021

This bottle contained 4 oz of Bovril, a salty meat and yeast extract paste which was developed by Scotsman, John Lawson Duncan, in the 1870s. This bottle has side seams on the diagonal and was manufactured by Forsters Glass Co from 1910 to around 1920, according to "The Society for Historical Archaeology."

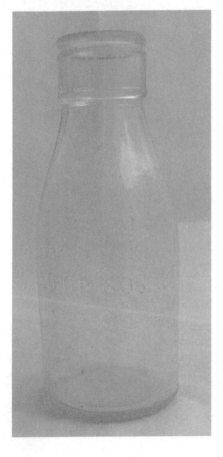

City of Perth
Co-op Society Milk Bottle
12 June 2021

This milk bottle is 15.5 cms high and holds 8 fluid ounces. It also has "Co-op milk is safer" embossed on the back of the bottle. It is too big to be a school milk bottle, so it is a bit of a puzzle.

The former City of Perth Co-operative building which dates from 1904-1906 is situated at 66-90 Scott Street, Perth.

Guild's Dairy Milk Bottle
October 2021

Guild's Dairy was situated at 41 Dundee Road West, Broughty Ferry, Dundee, in 1921. Sediment has collected in the neck of this bottle over the years and has completely hardened.

(Source: Friends of Dundee City Archives – Register of Milk Suppliers 1883-1922).

The site of the dairy is now occupied by an office building.

R R Randall & Co, Ryde
Summer 2021

This Codd neck bottle was found in the mud at low tide at Studland on the south coast of England by my eldest son. It is in good condition. It is quite unusual to find whole Codd neck bottles as they were usually broken in order to get the marble out of the neck.

Codd neck bottles were invented in 1872 by an engineer called Hiram Codd of Suffolk to address the problem of carbonated drinks losing their fizz. Codd's design solved this issue by using the pressure from the carbonated water to force the marble against a rubber washer in the upper ring of the bottle neck.

(Source: Glassing Magazine January/February 2018 issue) (Reproduced for beachcombingmagazine.com 21 March 2018)

R R Randall & Co, mineral water manufacturers, was started in the 1880s by Frank William Randall who was a chemist. According to the 1898 street directory, the company was situated in Church Lane, Ryde, on the Isle of Wight.

The join at the neck is clearly visible which dates it to around the 1880s.

(Source: Wikipedia)

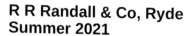

Lucozade Bottle and Stopper
December 2021

"Glucozade" was created in 1927 by William Hunter, a chemist from Newcastle. It was a mixture of glucose and carbonated water, hence the name. It was called Glucozade until 1938 when it was rebranded as Lucozade following its acquisition by Beechams, a pharmaceutical company.

(Source: suntorybeverageandfood-europe.com)

It was originally marketed as an aid to recovery from illness. Advertisements from the 1950s claimed it could "calm edgy nerves, put back vitality and gently stimulate the appetite."

The cost of a bottle then was 2 shillings and sixpence, plus a small deposit for the bottle.

It was also pretty much a standard feature on top of hospital lockers for many years!

By the 1980s it was rebranded from being a "health aid" to an energy booster and marketed as a sports drink in 1983.

MESSAGES IN BOTTLES

Message in a Bottle No 1
Photo by D McGurk

I found this bottle washed up on the beach at Buddon in August 2019. There was a sheet of laminated paper inside which told of a young man who had sadly passed away on 14 July 2019 after battling a brain tumour. There was an additional message which read "Please keep me floating out at sea, if you find me set me free." We put the paper back in and replaced the cork, then returned it to the sea. There was also a contact email for the person who had put the message in so we let her know that the bottle had been found.

Another poignant find at Buddon was a foil balloon with a message written by children who had lost their dad. They wished him a happy Christmas with the angels. It is just very unfortunate that these balloons and their strings are particularly dangerous for marine life as they look just like jellyfish floating along; a tasty snack with potentially fatal consequences once ingested. They frequently appear on the beach, some still full of helium even though they have been in the water long enough for all the pictures on them to have been rubbed off the surface.

Message in a Bottle No 2
21 March 2020

I was out walking on the beach at Buddon with my friend, Jacqui, just 2 days before the Corona Virus lockdown came into force. She had never been on this part of the beach before. I had been telling her of my various finds and in particular, the message in the bottle found in August 2019. The section of beach we were on was absolutely littered with bottles when we spotted this one, half buried in the sand behind a tree trunk, containing a message. We were both astonished by the sheer coincidence. As the cork was very firmly pushed in, I took the bottle home. It required a fair amount of effort, but we managed to ease it out. I then used long tweezers to get a hold of the message which was bound by raffia string. Some water had seeped in making the paper damp and unfortunately it did tear a bit but was still readable. I believe the language on the left-hand sheet to be either Latvian or Lithuanian. There is no date so it's anyone's guess as to how long it has been in the water or where it came from.

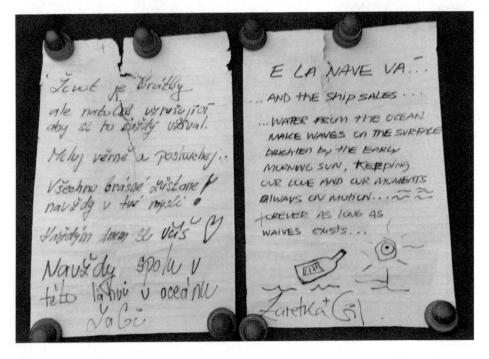

Message in a Bottle No 3
6 September 2020

I found this message in a bottle at Buddon in amongst a lot of plastic bottles which had been washed up in a particularly high tide. Inside the bottle there were 2 letters in envelopes with wax seals, some small pebbles, a 20p piece and a family photograph. There was a little water damage to the envelopes, but the letters were intact, one from Evie aged 7, who was in Primary 3 and her little sister, Tillie, who was in Primary 1. They lived in Auchtermuchty, Fife.

I wrote to Evie and Tillie to let them know where their bottle had been found.

Bottle 4 with Farmers Arms Hotel Business Card
2 January 2021

I found this bottle during our first beach clean of the year, towards the Buddon Burn.

Transcript:

HOUSE OF COMMERCIALS

The Farmers Arms Hotel

Prop J M Finch

Penny Street

Lancaster   Telephone

Back of card:

Fully Licensed

Restaurant	TV	Garage	Quality
Lunches	Teas	Dinners	with
Party Catering a Speciality			Comfort
H & C and Heating all Rooms			

At the beginning of the 20th century, 3 public houses, The White Cross Inn, The Corporation Arms and Prince William Henry, were demolished and rebuilt as 2 pubs; The Corporation Arms became the Farmers Arms with the White Cross next door. In the 1960s the White Cross and Farmers Arms were converted into a large public house and hotel, still bearing the Farmers Arms name. It closed in 2006 and in 2007 following a major refurbishment costing £2 M, reopened as Penny Street Bridge Hotel. In December 2015 it was redeveloped at a cost of £200,000 and renamed The Toll House Inn, which back in 1901, had been housed in the original Corporation Arms.

(Source: www.the visitor.co.uk Lancaster nostalgia)

Message in a Bottle No 5, Buddon
Summer 2021

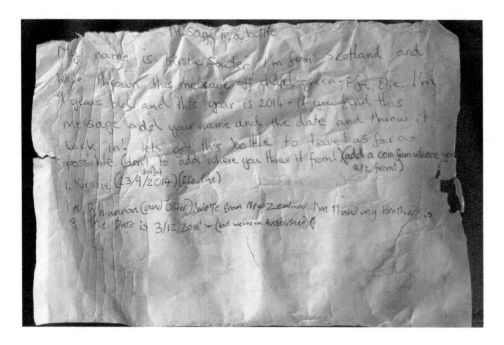

This message was in a plastic bottle and was thrown into the sea from Elie, Fife, in 2014 by Kirstie Soutar who was 9 at the time. It was subsequently found by Rhiannon (11) and Oliver (8) in Anstruther, Fife, on 3 December 2016. There was a 20p piece and a coin from New Zealand in the bottle as Rhiannon and Oliver were originally from New Zealand. Some water had started to leak into the bottle by the time I found it.

I have found several other bottles with messages in them and while it may, on the face of it be a fun and interesting thing to do, I have concluded that there is enough rubbish in the sea already without choosing to add any more. A few of the bottles have been thrown in from Broughty Ferry but only get as far as Buddon before being washed up.

VULCANISED RUBBER STOPPERS, GLASS/CERAMIC STOPPERS AND BOTTLE TOPS

Vulcanised rubber was patented by Charles Goodyear in 1846 but it wasn't until 1872 when Henry Barratt invented vulcanised rubber screw stoppers. The design was patented on 3rd August 1880. They were simple to mass produce and emboss the names of the firms on the top. They could also be reused, unlike corks, and would have kept the bottle contents from going flat.

Chisel shaped stoppers were brought out in 1885 by Frederick George Riley as they were designed to be easier to grip, either by hand or in a bottling machine.

(Source: tideline art blog)

During the Second World War, raw materials for manufacture were increasingly in short supply so in order to make them go as far as possible, the tops were scooped out. Some of the stoppers are marked "War Grade" and were probably made from poorer quality materials than their pre-war counterparts.

Robb Brothers Stopper
19 March 2020

I found this stopper, still inside the broken bottle neck and in very good condition. The brand of Bon Accord was originally sold under the Robb Brothers name, the company being founded in 1903 by Thomas and David Robb. They had factories in Arbroath and Aberdeen. The Bon Accord vans were a familiar sight, selling bottles of soft drinks around the streets in the 1960s. They closed in 2000 but reopened 16 years later.

(Source: Bon Accord Soft Drinks.com.history)

Murray, Craigmillar, Edinburgh
1 April 2020

Craigmillar Brewery was founded by William Murray at Ednam in 1880 and moved to Duddingston, Edinburgh, in 1886. It was acquired in 1960 by Northern Breweries of Great Britain and closed in 1963.

(Source: brewery history.com)

James Dunbar Ltd
1 April 2020 and 8 May 2020

James Dunbar Ltd was founded in 1868 at 14 Mayfield, Edinburgh, moving to Albion Road around 1911, manufacturing soft drinks and aerated water. It was taken over in the 1970s.

(Source: jamesdunbaredinburgh)

Ceramic Stoppers
21 April 2020

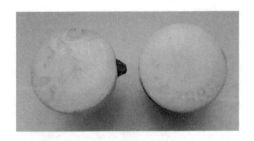

Ceramic stoppers were used with little wire clips to secure them onto the bottle neck. These particular stoppers came from James Jack, Pharmaceutical Chemist and Manufacturer of Aerated Mineral Waters, 102 High Street, Arbroath, according to the advertisement placed in the Arbroath Year Book 1926.

(Source: www.electricscotland.com)

McEwan's Stoppers
21 April 2020

William McEwan opened the Fountain Brewery in Fountainbridge, Edinburgh, in 1856. When the company was registered in 1889 it was the largest brewery in the UK under a single owner. In 1930 McEwan's merged with William Younger, forming Scottish Brewers. Scottish Brewers subsequently merged with Newcastle Breweries in 1960 to form Scottish & Newcastle.

(Source: Wikipedia)

Stillade Stoppers
28 April 2020

Stillade was manufactured in the late 1940s by John Robertson & Son of Dundee, Aberdeen, Perth and Dunfermline. Flavours included lime, grapefruit, orange, Scotch ginger and lemon. The advertising slogan was "Makes thirst a joy".

George Younger & Son, Alloa Stopper
29 April 2020

George Younger & Sons was founded in 1745 and they established the Meadow Brewery, Bank Street, Alloa, by 1764. They also leased the Candleriggs Brewery from 1852. The breweries were acquired by Northern Breweries of Great Britain Ltd in 1960, before ceasing brewing on 31 December 1963.

(Source: breweryhistory.com)

T Linsley & Co Ld, Hull, Stopper
30 April 2020

This stopper depicts the King William III equestrian statue in Market Place, Hull.

(Source: museumshull.blogspot.com)

The company was established in 1881 at Dagger Lane, Hull. It was acquired by Duncan Gilmour & Co of Sheffield in 1952.

(Source: The Brewing Industry: A Guide to Historical Records)

Sun Joy Stopper
1 May 2020

Sun Joy was manufactured by Co Ro Food, makers of fruit based uncarbonated soft drinks, based in Frederikssund, Denmark. The company was founded in 1942 and produced their goods in 11 countries. It was a popular drink in the 1960s.

(Source: Wikipedia)

Yardley Bottle Top
May 2020

This bottle top was kindly given to me by two of our beach clean team members after I said I collected them. The white stopper is made from Bakelite with a bumblebee on the top.

It was from a Yardley bottle from the 1950s containing moisturiser.

Lea and Perrins Bottle Neck and Glass Stopper
May 2020

Lea and Perrins Worcestershire sauce has been produced since 1837 when two chemists in Worcester, John Wheeley Lea and William Henry Perrins created a new condiment which had matured into a sauce after 18 months. It is exported to over 130 countries and is still manufactured in Worcester.

(Source: leaandperrins.co.uk)

It still has its little cork collar on the stopper to ensure an airtight seal, quite surprising given that it is over 100 years old and has clearly spent quite some time in the sea.

Kidd & Co/Tayport Stoppers
May 2020

Despite an extensive search, including looking at old Ordnance Survey maps, the only information I have been able to find was that the business of Kidd & Co, Dalgleish Street, Tayport, was dissolved on 31 January 1948.

(Source: jaglives.weebly.com/waterloo-tower-hunt)

The Design Registration Number, 696257 (as far as I can make out because it is abraded) indicates that it was registered between 1923-1924.

Crieff Aerated Water Co Stopper
13 June 2020

The Crieff Aerated Water Co was formed in 1892 and was based in West High Street, Crieff. The company was wound up in 1975.

(Source: archivescatalgue.pkc.gov.uk)

Flockhart & Co, Aberdeen Stopper
September 2020

Duncan Flockhart & Co were wholesale druggists, manufacturing chemists and aerated water manufacturers based at 104, 106 and 108 South Canongate, Edinburgh.

(Source: Scottish Post Office Directories 1911-1912)

The entry also notes that they were chemists to Her Late Majesty, Queen Victoria.

This particular stopper is dated 1934.

MacLennan, Belfast Stopper
23 September 2020

This stopper has "51" embossed on it so I assume this is dated 1951. The MacLennan Brewery Co Ltd was wound up in December 1983.

(Source: The Belfast Gazette, 25 November 1983).

The company was based at 468, 472 Castlereagh Road, Belfast.

(Source: The Belfast Gazette, 11 March 1983)

Glass Stoppers

These attractive glass stoppers were all found on the stretch of beach towards the Barry Buddon sentry post.

The most interesting stopper is the one marked "Gartons". Frederick Gibson Garton invented HP Sauce and patented it in 1896. He owned a small store where he sold his sauce. The recipe and brand were sold for £150 which also included a debt cancellation. In 1901, Tower Road, Aston Cross, became the registered office for the manufacture of "F G Garton's Sauce."

In 1903 it was relabelled as HP Sauce. This makes the Gartons bottle stopper at least 120 years old.

(Source: Grace's Guide to British Industrial History)

McLennan & Urquhart, Dalkeith
January 2020

The McLennan & Urquhart stopper still has some of the red rubber washer attached. The company was established in 1789 and registered in 1909. Brewing ceased in 1958 but bottling continued until 1961.

(Source: breweryhistory.com)

WCR & Co Ltd
November 2020

Watney Combe & Reid was a leading brewery in London, as a result of a merger in 1898 between James Watney & Co, Combe Delafield & Co and Reid & Co, thus becoming the largest brewery in London. There was a further merger with Mann, Crossman & Paulin Ltd in 1858, becoming Watney Mann. The leg on the "R" has been chipped off, making it look like a "P" instead.

(Source: Wikipedia and National Archives)

Drybrough & Co Ltd, Edinburgh
November 2020

I was given the WCR & Co Ltd stopper and the Drybrough & Co stopper by 2 of our regular Eco Force beach cleaners at our November Beach Clean. Drybrough & Co was an Edinburgh based brewery, operating from 1895 to 1987. They were taken over by Watney Mann (see above) in 1965 which I thought was a strange coincidence. The company was then bought over by Allied Lyons in 1987 who ended production the same year,

(Source: Wikipedia)

Aitken, Falkirk
22 January 2021

James Aitken's brewery was founded in Falkirk in 1740. The firm owned many pubs and was a major exporter of beers and stouts. Aitkens became part of Caledonian United Breweries in the 1960s, which in turn, was taken over by Tennents to form Tennent Caledonian a few years afterwards. Brewing finally ceased on the site in Newmarket Street in 1968 which is now occupied by a supermarket.

(Source: Falkirk Local History Society/Scottish Brewing Heritage)

John Dye Ltd, Arbroath/Montrose, G W Adamson, Methil, Trussell McIntyre & Co Ltd

I have been unable to find any information on these 3 manufacturers. If anyone has any details on these companies, I would be very grateful.

War Grade Stoppers

The middle stopper has been scooped out quite considerably. I think it would probably date to nearer the end of the Second World War when raw materials were in very short supply.

W A Willson, London SE "33"
6 March 2021

In spite of all the information on this stopper, I have drawn a blank on finding anything about this company, as have the mudlarks who have found similar stoppers on the banks of the River Thames. The 33 would indicate it was manufactured in 1933.

Deeply Scooped Barr stopper
18 March 2021

Most of the middle of this stopper has been scooped out, saving 25% of materials when compared to a normal stopper. There are also cracks round the rim which suggest that it is made from lower quality rubber. This evidence would suggest that it was probably manufactured in the latter stages of the Second World War or afterwards when raw materials were becoming increasingly scarce.

Franklin, Ricksmansworth
4 May 2021

This business was established in 1886 at 171 High Street, Rickmansworth, London, by George, Albert and Frederick Franklin. They brewed ginger beer and other soft drinks. The business was taken over by Frederick Franklin's son (also Frederick) in 1898 and was renamed Franklin & Sons.

In 1989 the company name disappeared following a takeover by a larger competitor but was subsequently relaunched in 2016.

(Source: diffordsguide.com)

Sangs, Aberdeen
28 June 2021

Sangs & Co began operating in 1896. It was listed in the Post Office Directory as a ginger beer manufacturer. The company was based at 1 Whitehall Place, Aberdeen.

(Source: emuseum.aberdeencity.gov.uk)

Anderson, Dundee
28 July 2021

This flat style stopper has "Anderson" embossed on one side and "Dundee" on the other, along with a registered design number 696257 on both sides indicating a date of 1924-1925. R J Anderson & Sons Ltd were manufacturers of "High-Class Mineral Waters, Unfermented Fruit Wines and Cordials" according to the advertisement placed in the Dundee Directory Advertisements in 1908-1909. The company was based at the Annfield Works, Dundee.

(Source: Scottish Post Office Directories 1908-1909)

Breadalbane Aerated
Water Co, Aberfeldy
23 January 2022

Breadalbane Aerated Water Company was owned by W & A Robertson Ltd, Aberfeldy, and produced Highland spring water in a range of fruit flavours according to an advertisement from the 1930s.

Wooden Stopper
6 February 2022

This wooden stopper, along with the original India rubber seal, is in remarkably good condition as it was found along with its bottle neck which has helped to preserve it. There are marks on the base from where the wood would have been held on the lathe while the top was being turned.

According to an advertisement placed in The Mineral Water Trade Supplement dated 17 August 1926, Lignumvitae Wood Screw Stoppers were introduced in the 1890s by a company called Harrison's. The Wood Turning Mills were at Bootle, Liverpool.

(Source: Advertisement reproduced in tidelineart.com)

Following the research into the bottles and stoppers, I was struck by how many independent breweries and drink manufacturers there were and how they gradually disappeared, being swallowed up by Scottish and Newcastle and other big breweries. I feel things have come full circle again with independent craft brewers and gin distillers now thriving.

It is an interesting reflection on changing tastes over the years. Most of the drinks bottles and vulcanised stoppers in my collection came from locally produced beers and ales, aerated water or soft drinks. Modern bottles washing up onto the beach now are more likely to be wine, vodka, rum and whisky and cider manufactured much further afield. I just fail to understand why people can carry a full bottle down to the beach but are then unable to take the empty one back to a bin or better still, a recycling point.

POTTERY

Maling Jar Base
8 August 2020

This was made by Maling which was a pottery founded in 1752 at North Hylton, near Sunderland. It subsequently moved to Newcastle-upon-Tyne in 1817 and closed in 1963.

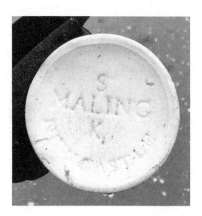

Maling supplied jars for James Keiller & Son, Dundee, for their marmalade. James Keiller & Son was established in 1828 and ceased trading in 1992. Janet Keiller (1787-1813), mother of James, who made the first commercial brand of marmalade is TV gardener and presenter Monty Don's great-great-great-great grandmother.

(Source: Wikipedia)

Wm Adams & Co Pottery Fragment

Wm Adams & Co was established in 1657, Tunstall, England. This particular piece was made for the American market (John Roth) in the 1900s. The business name John H Roth & Co came into being in 1909.

(Source: pottersmarks.blogspot.com)

PLASTIC

Much has been said about the scourge of plastic, especially in relation to the marine environment. It is quite difficult at times to walk along the beach and not feel overwhelmed and despondent about the sheer volume of plastic and other rubbish washed up.

Like the glass and pottery, it does provide a window into the past, albeit more recent.

Buddon
January 2021

During the first lockdown in early 2020 when all but essential businesses were closed, and movement was considerably restricted, there was an instant reduction in the number of wrappers and containers discarded from fast food outlets littering our pavements and beaches.

Unfortunately, it was only a temporary respite as once the takeaways reopened and people were able to get out and about, litter levels increased once again.

For some strange reason, I have found a lot of washing up liquid bottles. The Museum of Design in Plastics (MoDip) in Poole, was established in 1988 as a collection of objects for teaching and learning. Their online resource has been a useful tool in being able to date particular designs. These particular Sqezy bottles date from the 1960s. It would appear to have been a very popular brand over the years, judging by the various bottle designs and by the number I have found.

The oldest bottle which I found in September 2019 is branded "Doby". It was produced from 1953-1959. Other Doby branded bottles have been found as far away as Burnham-on-Sea, Somerset, in March 2019 and another in Lee-on-Solent, Hants, in 2018.

3 Hands Lightning Washing Up Liquid Bottle

This bottle pre-dates decimalisation (1971) with a price of 2 shillings and sixpence. In 1975 there was a strange advertisement on Irish television showing a man with 3 hands washing the dishes and extolling the benefits of this washing up liquid. If my memory serves me right, it was usually women and their daughters who featured in washing up liquid advertising. Men were nowhere to be seen.

(Source: ifiarchiveplayer)

The "Fairy" brand has also made it into the collection. One bottle commemorates the Queen's Jubilee. It could be the Silver Jubilee of 1977 as it has clearly been around for quite some time.

Jubilee Bottle
Fairy Bottle 6D Off

I found this bottle on a coastal walk from Kingsbarns to Crail in November 2020. It is still in very good condition, despite being at least 50 years old as it has 6D off the price. Decimalisation took place on 15 February 1971.

Wm Low Bottle

On a more local note, I found a Wm Low washing up liquid bottle in November 2019. Wm Low was a supermarket chain which was based in Dundee. It was taken over by Tesco in 1994 which means the bottle is at least 26 years old.

Fine Fare Bottle

Fine Fare started out in the 1950s as a chain of convenience stores and grew into a supermarket chain. It was bought out by the Dee Corporation in 1986. The last Fine Fare store closed in 1988.

(Source: Simply Eighties)

An Unholy Trinity Booker, Fairy and Fine Fare Bottles 27 March 2020

I found these bottles all fairly close to each other at the mouth of the Buddon Burn. The Booker (a cash and carry business) and Fairy bottles are relatively recent as they are metric, but the Fine Fare bottle is marked with both metric and imperial measurements.

We may have had very clean dishes for the last 70 years but environmentally we are now paying a very high price with what has ended up in our seas and landfill, prior to plastic recycling being introduced.

Red Nose
September 2019

The list for plastic waste could go on forever. Who would have thought that a red plastic nose bought as a fundraiser for the original Red Nose Day in 1988 would wash up on a beach, relatively intact, 31 years later? Red noses are now manufactured from bio degradable materials, so they will not be turning up intact decades down the line.

Marathon Wrapper
April 2020

For those of us old enough to remember Marathon chocolate bars before they were renamed "Snickers" in 1990!

Crisp packets would appear to be pretty indestructible. The KP Crispi Meanies Pickled Onion packet has a BBE 18 Jan 1992 and cost 6p! The Golden Wonder packet is even older as it had a closing date of 26 June 1981 for sending in tokens, ironically to support the World Wildlife Fund.

KP Crisp Packet
October 2019

The best before date on this crisp packet is 7 July 1984.

Golden Wonder Packet
March 2020

Ropes and discarded fishing nets have been well documented as extremely dangerous, especially to larger marine mammals. One such collection of rope caught in the rock armour took my younger son, Kieran, and I three quarters of an hour to cut through, then another 2 adults to help us to haul it up the steps from the beach to the collection point.

A dead adult seal was found at Lunan Bay in August 2020 with a length of rope wrapped right round its front flippers and along towards the rear flippers, a heartbreaking sight.

Rope Flower Bed,
Beach Garden, Monifieth

This length of rope was reused to make a raised flower bed on top of an old tree stump at the Beach Garden beside the Bowling Pavilion in Monifieth, rather than ending up in a landfill site.

Mooring Rope
February 2020

Frisbees

Dog toys are frequently washed up. Our Border Collie, Shelby, now has a collection of tennis balls that a tennis club might be proud of. Various other types of balls and toys appear, including ping pong balls, footballs and golf balls.

Probably the most dangerous of all, particularly for seals, are frisbees like the ones above as small seal pups can get their heads through the hole. Unfortunately, they cannot get them off and as the seal grows, the frisbees become embedded in the flesh, with devastating consequences for the seal unless they are spotted in time, caught, and given intensive veterinary treatment.

If you find a frisbee, please pick it up and dispose of it carefully. Perhaps the safest thing to do is not to take frisbees to the beach so that they cannot be left behind.

Children's toys also make a regular appearance on the beach. On 2 consecutive cleans at Buddon, Little Tikes Cozy Coupe cars were removed. At the February 2020 Eco Force beach clean, some young children toiled to dig out a pink plastic scooter which was partially buried in the sand.

One day in September 2019, I was surprised to come across a very large toy dog lying flat on its back on the beach at Barnhill. Shelby is beside it to give an idea of the size.

Sometimes I find dolls, like the ones pictured below, looking slightly creepy. Other times it may be just arms and legs or a head. Something for the Silent Witness team to investigate? Dolls always seem to end up lying on their backs when they are washed up.

Kellogg's "Snap" Figure, Dated 1990

This is a pencil topper which would have been in a pack of Kellogg's Rice Krispies. The other figures to collect are "Crackle" and "Pop". Snap made his first appearance on Rice Krispies packaging in 1933 before being joined by Crackle and Pop.

(Source: Wikipedia)

Plastic Soo Figure
November 2020

This is part of a set which were given away in boxes of Kellogg's cereals around 1970, the other figures being Sooty, Sweep, Kipper and Butch and were available in different colours.

(Source: WorthPoint)

Road cones, tyres, wheels and temporary barriers regularly wash up.

Tyres and Cones
May 2019

This impressive haul was collected from the section of beach between the sentry point beside the Tayview Caravan site and the Buddon Burn.

Shelby and Tractor Tyre Barnhill, Broughty Ferry, January 2020

At the other end of the spectrum is small plastic. Cotton bud sticks are found everywhere along our beaches as they manage to get through the filtration systems at the sewage treatment works, even though they should be binned instead of being flushed down toilets. Manufacturers have now switched to paper instead of plastic as legislation banning plastic cotton bud sticks had been due to come in from April 2020. It was delayed because of the Covid 19 pandemic but the legislation was finally enacted on 1 October 2020. Unfortunately, I fear we will be picking up plastic sticks from our beaches for many years to come in spite of this.

Fishing Net
25 February 2020

I found this very large section of fishing net just beside the outfall for the Monifieth Burn. The risk of entanglement to marine life doesn't bear thinking about. It was quite a challenge to get it to the bin so that it could be safely disposed of.

At the opposite end of the scale, monofilament fishing line and lures with hooks are also extremely dangerous both in the sea and once washed up onto the shoreline.

Discarded fishing gear is a huge problem all-round the coastline. The community at Easthaven further along the coast from Carnoustie used to have a collection point for nets, creels, buoys, fish boxes and other fishing gear removed from the beach with a view to retrieval and re-use.

McDonald's Toy
13 June 2020

I found this ghastly creature on one of our many "lockdown" walks along Buddon. Once it was cleaned, the writing on the back revealed that it is a 2020 McDonald's toy.

In 2019, two girls, Ella, 10 and Caitlin, 8, instigated a petition through the *change.org* platform to ask McDonalds and Burger King to stop giving out plastic toys with Happy Meals. The petition gained 568,162 signatures.

On 27 March 2020, McDonalds UK and Ireland responded to the petition to say that they would only include soft toys, sustainable paper gifts or books from 2021, thereby removing over 3,000 tonnes of non-sustainable plastic from the environment. Plastic wrapping on gifts will also be removed, saving another 200 tonnes of plastic.

Thank you and well done to Ella and Caitlin.

McDonalds Trolls
Summer 2021

Once lockdown had been eased and people could travel a bit more freely, the beach became a very popular destination for a day out. Unfortunately, it also became a dumping ground for plastic toys and more McDonalds monstrosities which had been played with for perhaps all of 10 minutes before being left on the beach. Although it was good to see people enjoying being outdoors again, it was disheartening to witness the amount of rubbish being left behind including crisp packets, reusable bottles and cups (!), toys, food, single use barbecues, towels, face masks and bottles of hand sanitiser. The abandoned toys were given to a local nursery rather than going in the bin. Electronic cigarettes are now appearing on the beach and elsewhere. They are doubly hazardous due to the fact they are plastic and also because of the electronic element which will corrode in seawater.

Smashed Up Glass
July 2020

During a walk along the beach at Buddon I was absolutely horrified to discover that someone had gone along at least a 100 metre stretch of beach, systemically smashing up pretty every single glass bottle they could find. Incandescent doesn't even come close to how I felt.

It is beyond mindless and a huge hazard to people, animals and ultimately to marine life once there is a high enough tide to sweep it all back out to sea. Due to the Covid 19 pandemic, both the scheduled Buddon 2020 cleans for April and September, in conjunction with Monifieth Rotary Club, were cancelled. Our usual monthly beach cleans were also temporarily halted until restrictions were relaxed enough to allow a few volunteers to attend.

As a postscript to this, Shelby was injured in November 2020 after slicing one of her pads at Buddon so badly that the vet had to remove the damaged part completely. She had a week bandaged up, 3 days of painkillers and several trips to the vet as a result. Our wildlife is not afforded this care if they get hurt.

As a consequence of the ongoing restrictions due to Covid 19 in 2020, there were no organised bonfire nights and firework displays so people resorted to their buying their own. Unfortunately, whoever decided to have their displays on the beach did not bother to tidy up afterwards so the beach cleaners who turned up on the Saturday following the 5th of November cleared up the boxes, rockets, Roman candles and sticks. We also had a repeat performance in November 2021 with dozens of spent fireworks littering the beach. At the New Year's Day beach clean in 2022, we also retrieved 2 big boxes of fireworks which had been detonated at the Blue Seaway park beside the beach plus more firework related debris from the beach.

Several petitions have been submitted to Parliament over the past couple of years regarding the availability of fireworks to the general public, some of which have called for an outright ban on supply unless for organised displays. The Government

Response on 25 November 2021 stated that "We believe the majority of people who use fireworks do so responsibly. The Government also believes that the current legislation strikes the right balance allowing people to enjoy fireworks, whilst reducing the risks and disturbances to both people and animals. There are, however, strong enforcement mechanisms in place to tackle situations where fireworks are used inappropriately. Given this, the Government has no current plans to introduce further restrictions on the sale of fireworks to the public, but we continue to monitor the situation."

(Source: parallelparliament.co.uk)

I would beg to differ with this view. However, on 1 February 2022, the Fireworks and Pyrotechnic Articles (Scotland) Bill was introduced in the Scottish Parliament. The bill became law on 29 June 2022 which means it is now an offence to buy fireworks without a licence or let them off in "firework control zones" as designated by local authorities. Time will tell if this legislation will make a difference.

Buddon Beach Clean
September 2021

As Covid 19 restrictions were finally relaxed enough to allow a Buddon Clean in September 2021, it was cheering to see how many volunteers turned out to help. The event was also supported by representatives from Angus Clean Environment (ACE) who weighed and catalogued what had been collected.

Around 602 kg of rubbish was removed, including 49 kg of fishing net, an HGV tyre, 2 car bumpers, 3 traffic cones and 59 bags of mixed waste as well as 14 oil type canisters containing an unknown substance.

UNUSUAL FINDS

During the Buddon clean in 2018 we found a
Go Pro type camera, still in its watertight box.
We took it home and retrieved the memory card
which showed a group of teenagers having fun
in a river. The footage only lasted a few minutes
before it cut to what was clearly the riverbed, after
which it stopped recording. The date stamp on
the film was 2016 which is testament to the dura-
bility of the casing.

November 2018

A military radio in a waterproof pouch was found at the same beach clean, probably accidentally dropped during the exercises which regularly take place off the
Angus coastline.

26 December 2018
Photo by Kevin McGurk

There is also a boat which is buried upside down in the sand quite a way along from the lighthouses at Barry Buddon, heading towards Carnoustie. It has a fibreglass hull and depending on the tides and sand, nearly vanishes then reappears. It doesn't appear to have a name or any identifiable markings, so it is a mystery as to where it came from. My sons and I partially excavated it on Boxing Day 2018 – a great way to work off Christmas excesses.

Drone
August 2019

As can be seen from the size of the posts it was sitting on, it was quite sizeable.

Wood with SNCF Badge
October 2019

I was very surprised to find this piece of wood bearing the SNCF badge washed up in Monifieth. The Societe Nationale de Chemins de Fer Francais is France's national state-owned railway company. It was founded in 1938.

(Source: www.britannica.com)

July 1935 Carved Wood
12 February 2020

I found this piece of wood quite by accident. I had been ready to head for home after a walk along to the Buddon Burn but Shelby had other ideas and ran onto the beach on the other side of the Monifieth Burn where this was lying.

It looks like a piece of root which has been sliced horizontally with Jul 1935 carved on the face. I wonder where it came from, who took the time to carve it and what it commemorated. It is a very tactile piece and I treasure it.

Mother of Pearl Button
June 2020

This pretty button is now very thin and abraded. I think it has spent quite some time in the sea.

"Poison" Glass Fragment
10 July 2020

The Victorians seem to have been very partial to poisons, judging by the vast array of bottles on the internet. This fragment is rather unusual, being in clear glass – most bottles containing poisons were in blue or green glass.

Letter Opener Handle
November 2020

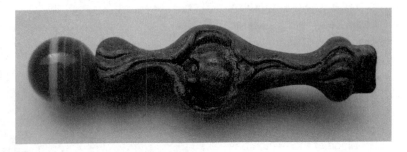

This bronze handle has a polished round agate on top. Unfortunately, the blade section is missing. It was kindly given to me by two of the Eco Force beach clean team.

Television Set
Buddon, November 2020

I have often complained about the amount of rubbish on the television. I did not expect a television to be part of the rubbish. This was washed up after a particularly high tide in November.

"Viking" Longship
Carnoustie, November 2020

I was rather surprised to find this "ship" rolling about on the tideline at Carnoustie at the end of November. It was made of chipboard and was partly burnt out, with a cable running along the side of it and screws sticking out, not exactly the most seaworthy vessel ever. As it was quite unwieldy I was only able to haul it clear of the high-water mark.

It was finally completely removed during the fourth Great Angus Beach Clean in May 2021.

Plastic Tina Onassis Ship
Buddon, 25 December 2020

I found this little plastic ship, just over 6 cms long, at Buddon on Christmas Day 2020. The original Tina Onassis ship was a chemical/oil tanker which was built by HDW Hamburg in Germany in 1953, gross tonnage 28,798 tons. Her current status is decommissioned/lost.

(Source: balticshipping.com)

She was, at the time, the biggest tanker in the world. She was named 'Tina Onassis' after the wife of the owner Aristotle Onassis, the Greek shipping magnate (1906-1975).

(Source: greekshippinghalloffame.org)

Glass Insulator
11 July 2021, Buddon

This insulator is a CD164 and was produced from the 1880s through to the 1940s before being replaced by the CD165. It was used for carrying telegraph wires.

(Source: hemingway.net)

The only clue as to the manufacturer of this insulator is a horizontal diamond on the side. It would appear that it was made by the Diamond Glass Co, Manitoba, Canada.

(Source: sha.org)

Earthenware Pot
September 2021,
Buddon Beach Clean

This earthenware pot is only 4.5 cms high and is glazed inside and out. There are no maker's marks. It may have contained ointment and would have been sealed with a cork stopper.

Chair, Buddon
February 2021

I was sorely tempted to take this garden chair home but unfortunately it was very heavy, and we were about 3 miles from the car. I think someone else had the same idea because it had disappeared by the time we came back along the beach.

Stone sculptures, Barnhill
April 2021

Someone had been busy creating these attractive stone sculptures. It certainly made a welcome change from looking at piles of rubbish.

Pebble, Barnhill
1 April 2021

This was quite an apt find for April Fool's Day!

NATURE

False Killer Whale Jawbone

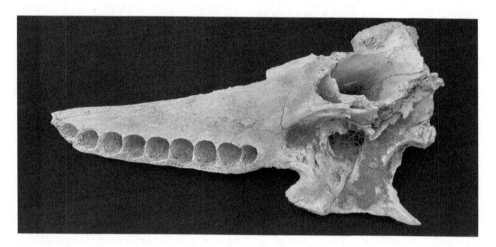

I found this section of upper jawbone sticking out of the sand during a beach clean in 2013. I had no idea what it was from initially, but further research has shown that 42 False Killer Whales had stranded at Carnoustie on 27 November 1935.

(Source: Natural History Museum (2018); Dataset: Historical UK cetacean strandings dataset (1913-1989) Natural History Museum Data Portal (data.nhm. ac.uk)

The bodies were subsequently buried at Buddon so the best guess is that the section of jawbone had washed up from there. The pod comprised 19 males, the largest of which was 18'8"/5.59 m. The females were smaller, ranging from 13'/3.96 m to 15'7"/4.7 m. Two younger orcas, a male and a female, were around 9'4'/2.84 m.

The jawbone is 41 cms long and the tooth sockets are 3 cms wide. It weighs 1.5 kg.

Shells

There is a wide variety of shells to be found on the beach. It is unusual to find such a large dog whelk (top right) unbroken and not carrying barnacle passengers.

April 2020

On 22 March 2018 a 45-foot sperm whale became stranded on the beach in Monifieth. In spite of the best efforts from British Divers Marine Life Rescue (BDMLR), HM Coastguard and the Broughty Ferry lifeboat crew, there was nothing to be done to help the whale and it sadly died. A post mortem, along with tissue sampling was carried out by teams from the Scottish Marine Animal Stranding Scheme (SMASS), staff and students from St Andrew's Sea Mammal Research Unit and BDMLR volunteers, before the whale was buried on the beach.

Unfortunately, some of the remains are exposed at low tide and the smell emanating from them is absolutely revolting if you have the misfortune to be down wind of it. Dogs, on the other hand, have been very drawn to the decomposing flesh and have thoroughly enjoyed a good roll in it, much to the disgust of their owners. The sand beside the whale has gas bubbles popping up to the surface from decomposition of the flesh. Signs were erected on either side of the remains warning people to keep away from the burial site but Storm Ciara which struck in February 2020 ripped the signs out completely.

They were subsequently replaced but Storm Barra at the beginning of December 2021 which came hard on the heels of Storm Arwen, took the signs out once more.

Seal Pup
November 2019

My husband, Shelby and I were out for a walk at Buddon. It was quite a windy day with a very high tide. We were quite a way along the beach towards Carnoustie when we came across this young seal pup, lying beside a tree with its eyes closed. I initially thought it was dead but as I approached it, its eyes opened, and it attempted to wriggle down to the beach. The tide was turning to go out, but the waves were very high and there was no sign of an adult anywhere.

We were able to contact British Divers Marine Life Rescue (BDMLR) and gave them the location and condition of the pup. We were soaked through by the time we got home, and it was starting to get dark. Later on, BDMLR contacted us to say that they had managed to collect the seal and that it was on its way to the Scottish Society for Prevention of Cruelty to Animals (SSPCA), National Wildlife Rescue Centre, near Alloa, to be cared for until being fit enough to be released.

If you find a live stranded marine mammal, contact British Divers Marine Life Rescue on 01825 765546 which is a 24-hour rescue hotline. If a seal is stranded or injured, please keep people and dogs clear. Do not approach the seal or try to put it back in the water.

If you find a stranded dolphin, porpoise or a whale, BDMLR guidance is to keep the animal upright and keep it wet but avoid water going down the blowhole. Do not attempt to refloat it. Avoid contact with the animal's breath as this can contain harmful pathogens. Further information is available at www.BDMLR.org.uk.

Beaver Skull and Beaver Tree
December 2019

This beaver skull was found by Ben Lawrie, a local councillor, during the Eco Force December beach clean. I am finding increasing numbers of trees on the beach which have been felled by beavers living further up the Tay and washing down river. Beavers are now protected by law so neatly chiselled trees washing down river and onto the beach will become even more common as beaver numbers rise. There are also beavers living in the Dighty Burn, upstream from the Seven Arches Viaduct in Monifieth.

Cowrie Jar

This jar of cowries came from Michael's shed at Westhaven when he sold it in the late 1980s. They had been collected from the beach over the course of many years. One day, during the school holidays when we were staying at Carnoustie, my sister and I decided to count them so we all had a guess as to how many were in the jar.

Michael put up a small prize for the nearest guess. We were all a long way off with the first guess, but Lindsay won as she guessed highest so we all had another turn. Three guesses later, the cowries were all counted, and Lindsay was better off as she won every guess. It certainly kept us occupied for quite some time.

Despite many hours spent on the beach at Monifieth, I have only managed to find one cowrie which now lives in my jewellery box. It is the one beside the jar.

Porpoise Skull
April 2020

I found this piece of skull at Buddon. It was much more fragile than I expected it to be.

Dolphin Vertebrae

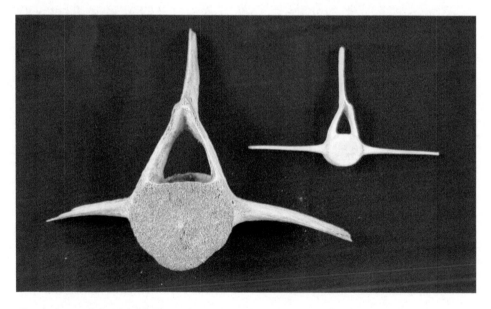

The larger of the 2 vertebrae is 25 cms across and 20 cms high. It would have been wider and taller, but the ends of the bones have been broken off from being tumbled about. The smaller one is in much better condition and is 16 cms across and 10 cms tall.

11 February 2021

This snowman was on the beach following very heavy snow in February.

TINY FINDS

This eclectic mix includes a tiny plastic shoe, Garfield, a rubbery unicorn and a little duck which I think has escaped from a duck race as it has the number 5 on its head.

BREWERS AND DRINKS MANUFACTURERS

Aitken, Falkirk
Ballingall Brewers, Dundee
Ballingall & Son Ltd, Glasgow
Barr, Wishaw & Irvine, Glasgow
Breadalbane Aerated Water Co,
    Aberfeldy
Campbell & Co, Forfar
Calder, Alloa
Crieff Aerated Water Co
D & W Edwards, Broughty Ferry
David Nicoll, Fleuchar Craig, Dundee
Drybrough, Edinburgh
Flockhart & Co, Aberdeen
Fowler, Prestonpans
Franklin, Rickmansworth, London
Garvie, Milngavie
G & P Barrie, Dundee and Glasgow
G & P Millar, Perth
G W Adamson, Methil
G Thomson & Son, Falkirk, Airdrie,
    Dysart
George Younger & Son, Alloa
Hays, Aberdeen/Inverurie
Jack, Arbroath
Jas Dunbar Ltd, Albion Road,
    Edinburgh
John Campbell Ltd, Perth
John Robertson & Son, Dundee &
    Perth
Dunn, Glasgow
John Dye Ltd, Montrose/Arbroath
Johnston Hill & Co Ltd, Dumfries
Kidd & Co, Tayport

Lambs, Strathmore Springs, Forfar
Lucozade, Newcastle
McEwans, Edinburgh
McLennan, Belfast
McLennan & Urquhart Ltd, Dalkeith
M Grubb, Dysart
M & M Aberdeen
Melville & Co, Dundee
Mitchell, Dunfermline and Bathgate
Murray, Craigmillar, Edinburgh
R Douglas Ltd, Kirkcaldy and
    Dunfermline
R J Anderson & Sons Ltd, Dundee
R R Randall, Ryde, Isle of Wight
Robert Barr Ltd, Falkirk
Robert Younger Ltd, Edinburgh
Robb Brothers, Arbroath and
    Aberdeen
Robertson Fruit Products Ltd, Dundee
Sangs, Aberdeen
Scottish Brewers Ltd, Edinburgh
Strathmore Springs, Forfar
Sun Joy, Denmark
T Linsley & Co, Hull
The Newcastle Breweries Ltd
Thomson, Craik & Co, Perth
Trussell McIntyre & Co Ltd
W A Willson, London SE
Walkers Whisky, Kilmarnock
WCR & Co Ltd, London
Whitbread & Co, London
Wright, Perth
Usher, Edinburgh

AUTHOR BIO

From childhood I have always enjoyed being beside the sea and beaches. I have been fortunate to live in Monifieth on the Angus coast for nearly 30 years with easy access to many beautiful beaches such as Monifieth, Buddon, Carnoustie, Arbroath, Auchmithie, Lunan Bay and Montrose heading up the east coast with Tentsmuir, Kinshaldy, St Andrews and all the beaches round the East Neuk of Fife to the south. They are all different, some have miles of sand, others are rocky, and some are covered in pebbles. Our whole family has enjoyed many walks and holidays beside the sea in North Yorkshire, Wales and the West Coast of Scotland. They all hold a wealth of happy memories.

I have been proud to support Monifieth Eco Force in their efforts over the past decade to improve the local environment. Taking care of the world we live in now is more important than it ever was. We can all make a difference.

I can be contacted via email: *seonaidmcgurk@gmail.com*

Printed in Great Britain
by Amazon

10967482R00059